FORCEHYMN

To Richard —
your Pal —

Tom —

10.19.84

BY THE SAME AUTHOR

This Life: A Salutation.
 Thorp Springs Press, Chapel Hill, 1975.
Sixteen People Who Live Downtown, a Novel
 Coraddi Press, Greensboro, 1979.

TOM HUEY

FORCEHYMN

CAROLINA WREN PRESS
Chapel Hill, North Carolina
1979

ACKNOWLEDGEMENT

Section 37 of *Forcehymn* appeared in the
Spring, 1977 issue of *International Poetry Review*.
Many thanks to Evelyn Gill, editor,
for permission to reprint.

Library of Congress Cataloging in Publication Data

Huey, Tom, 1950–
 Foreehymn : a poem.

 I. Title.
PS3558.U317F6   811'.5'4   78-24417
ISBN 0-932112-05-6

MEMBER
COSMEP
COMMITTEE OF SMALL MAGAZINE
EDITORS AND PUBLISHERS
BOX 703 SAN FRANCISCO, CA. 94101

FORCEHYMN

Introduction
by Fred Chappell

FORCEHYMN

THE IDLER'S WHEELS

LOVE IN RETURN

INTRODUCTION

Sometimes there rises before me, as Erda to the Wanderer, an image: of a slightly retarded, hugely and softly obese man, sitting, sitting with his thumb up his smugness, licking his dollars. And this image does not signify the broad unintriguable American public, but the smaller yet equally over-hyped community of American poets.

For when Amon Liner died in 1976, he disappeared without stirring a flutter in the dovecote of American letters. Amon Liner was the most brilliant technical innovator since Ezra Pound, and in his subject matter one of the most courageous poets since Browning. I make these claims soberly and responsibly, having lived with his first book, *Marstower*, since 1972, and with his second book, *Chrome Grass*, since it was published in the week that he died. When I say "lived with," I mean that no month has passed that I have not looked into one of these books with wonder and admiration.

He did not write an easy poetry, but one that is — at first glance — formidable and uninviting. But it is the duty of poets to care for poetry, to look into it, to see what is there, and to get it before whatever public they can in whatever way they can. Yet in Liner's case they have not and do not; because poets are too busy with those spoiled little pets their Reputations, feeding them bonbons and grooming them with eau de cologne.

I can write no further on this subject; despair choketh me and rage prevaileth.

Herewith now, *Forcehymn*, Tom Huey's poem which to a large degree was occasioned by Amon Liner's death.

We know how Rilke, after spending ten years composing the *Duino Elegies*, wrote down the 55 *Sonnets to Orpheus* in two weeks in February, 1922. The occasion was the death of a dancer, the daughter of his friend, a 19-year-old girl. This spectacle of the too-early death of the young and brilliant is likely to draw from the poet — almost without his willing them — the profoundest and most intense responses. So it was too with Shelley's *Adonais*.

These terribly earnest responses seem to follow a pattern, perhaps they are partly ritualized. The surviving poet sees it as his task first to fix an image of his departed friend, rescuing that personality from the onrush of time; then next to set the departed one in a future cultural milieu which he may have helped to refashion; then next to try to define that vision, perhaps even to try to see in that manner of seeing. But the hardest part of the job will be personal, in defining the speaker's relationship to the dead man and his living vision. The speaking poet must come to terms with the catastrophe; he must return to a life which now includes that death, and he must find meaning in both. Now is the poet a bridge between the dead and the living, the past and the future.

These ritual needs and hungers determine the three-part structure of *Forcehymn*. The first part, from which the whole volume takes its title, deals with the shock of the death itself, taking place over the long night after the event and during the following day. The funeral is remembered in the familiar guilty terms we all feel, "All the way I can't forget how I couldn't pass even one holy look to your immediate family." There is the attempt to hold down an image of Liner both as person ("dead man, who are you?") and as poet ("I know a man who died touching everything closed"). In trying to fix the poet, the speaker is necessarily led into an examination of a poet's vocation: its doubleness ("My right eye's cool, my left warm") and its danger ("The stakes were high, the fires red and horse-rent flesh later rooted in the cracked streets"). The case of Liner is particularly difficult because of the revolutionary nature of his art; the speaker finds it hard to bring his "human" memories in line with the unpitying principles of his friend's work. "Is the mind-tree more real than a past crime or the world a cage we have to craft closed, accepting?"

The metaphor of the journey, the pilgrimage, is often a central one in this kind of poetry; it is a quest for reconciliation. The second part of *Forcehymn*, "The Idler's Wheels," is taken up with a long, seemingly aimless, drive in a car. The driving metaphor is particularly apt because it allows us to see the contemporary landscape in the terms that Liner saw it; ashen and harrowing, it is not an engaging spectacle. And the great web of traffic on the crumbling highways allows a set of secondary metaphors — information "bits" shuttling through computers, corpuscles in the bloodstream, and so forth — directly alluding to the subject matter of Liner's verse. But beyond this, it represents the poet's attempt to broaden his personal sorrow into a historical context. Mr. Huey experiments in this section with trying to see his autobiography in cultural terms, in terms of the milieu in which he lives. One of the most difficult of all tasks for the artist. Then, after an inevitable comparison of Liner with the "I" of the poem, comes the determination to survive in the world, *the world as Liner imaged it out*. This deliberate acceptance of, inclusion of, the vision of another poet in one's own work stands among the rarest accomplishments in verse. To include the vision of another, without becoming a disciple or an imitator, requires equally inordinate reserves of skill and will power.

The final section, "Love in Return," may startle readers. It is rather as if a composer, after having written the first two movements of a sonata in the modern, anguished, and dissonant style, should compose the third movement in simple chorale-like harmonies and modulations. "Love in Return" is a series of poems addressed to, or about, the poet's love for his wife and his domestic life. In one sense, this is an eminently satisfactory resolution, since it does give reason for and hope to the poet's personal existence in the absence of his friend. But in another way it might be found an evasion of responsibility, since it can answer none of the philosophical problems raised by Liner's work. Truly, though, there is no attempt at evasion here, but a thoughtful attempt at transcendence. The specter of an uncommunicative loveless society might be laid by a wholehearted devotion to a living person. In his person as the lover the speaker may overcome the more destructive characteristics of the culture he inhabits; he must be whole himself before he can offer healing counsel. The more intellectual problems (always for a poet the *lesser*) he may address in his later work. — For me, "Love in Return" is a successful resolution; its daringness, as well as its simplicity, is tonic.

Here then is *Forcehymn*, elegy, meditation, and love poem. I am not surprised, looking back over this broken bit of introduction, to find that I have done it so little justice. It is an uncompromising and complex work, containing more thought and more feeling and intention than any short piece can profitably examine. Let it now present itself to the unhurried reader that he may muse, speculate, and admire.

— *Fred Chappell*
Greensboro, North Carolina

I

FORCEHYMN

This poem is dedicated to the memory of Amon Liner, whose poetry will last much longer than he or I.

> *"His every step skirts
> reality; his tender mode of
> discourse is silence."*

FORCEHYMN

Post mortem:

Old Guy Turned Wolf awoke on the plain after great
destruction of life. The flax and wildgrass were red
as far as he could see. When he turned skyward
for words with the flying souls he unexpectedly found himself
looking at Holiest One's asshole. This he said without
thinking: "Why do you come here dirty and low?"
Holiest One's wind put out tent fires as far as the
nearest bloody sun. It's said Old Guy's women forgot
how to raise natural children and dream for three score.
I walk on the plain after no destruction of life. Heaven
is still sky, but after so much death what could happen?

1

Free from death and the dying, I move to your grave.
Surrounded by the dead, remembering your life,
I move to clear the plastic flowers before they ruin my
own short sleep.
I have dreamed of this, before your death, perhaps before my life.
I have seen the easy way around weeping, the logic, and
called it faith.
I have skirted a thousand star-possibilities for the sake of breath.
But when it comes to this, when it can no longer come to you,
I know there is such a thing as ageless sorrow, when a man
can cry without tears even longer than his life
and see into his past and future the same crying waters.
How they move as one circle, friend. Let me move to you!

2

You cannot turn from your own death, though you would like to,
like a wrong word not needed but thought, like a wrong street
dreamed but walked anyway. You cannot turn from a friend's
death, though you would like to, like a friend you saw turning
from himself . . . and you told him, and he told you: You cannot
turn from anything but your shoulder and in the end it meets the
circle you've been trying to chalk the whole time; you cannot turn
from death or friends or circles or chalk or anything, or even
nothing, for everything, including nothing, meets you head-on
no matter where your head is turning, meets you like the shoulder
you never see, like the shoulder that's there, turning . . .

3

Blue-green through sunless highway haze. In sunless
space blue-green replaces the jet one star past sunset:
more room for hard eyes to ease down after that vision,
more room to go blinder than before, to lose. How *bad*
this sounds—the sinking soul, the whine. Give me
what I've become and I'll go with it in this blue-green
place called
world, where silences meet separations, where void
rolls to indifference and nothing changes or happens
more than it ever could. Self-deception, may you
remain where the sunless haze envelops our old shadows.

4

Why do I wait for you tonight? What remains of you
but this hot collision of brain and fuzz and no chance to
wind down before morning? When you didn't belong in
the world but remained like no one before to sample each
discord and delight separately, carefully, did you ever
see what you had left, or been loosed from partially,
or would find as if you had never lost it at all? We
never talked about that. The future concerned us because
it was all we had. Where we'd been was cornerstone for
what we'd build. What we'd need was love and a few
open windows. Nights, we determined, were best for final views.

5

Were you a channel upon which pyres would float
like blossoms into the belly of sorrow I would leave
the beach and salt my romantic tongue on your touch.
But you swallow every vanity like the ocean—I can't
wave you back or see where you're going. What have
we become so hard in its distance we can't
reach across? I won't wait like Samson for falling
columns. There's too much left at sea for drowning
reminders, too much rising, and a surface so great
without it I'd feel left behind. But if once, right
here, you could see this late-day grayness swell. . . .

6

He spoke of you as if the truth is learned from the
very, very tired; and he would try, no matter if it
killed him, to compare you not to a summer's day (which
you were) but to a "lamplighter." Somehow, this saved
me. I smiled inside and so did you. The lamplighter,
lighting, lit the tired preacher's way and when it was
over I put out a few lamps myself. The one called
memory I let flicker because it was safe under two
years of steady love; the other, including pain and the
absence of love, I simply stopped watching. Who
needs fire on an already burned-out trail through July?

7

Every flower must hate needlepoint. The miracle
is no control over sunrise yet. Let the smoke lose its shape
over a morning intersected by steeples!
Five-hundred churches cannot conspire to build a holy network
strong enough to capture death rising! I follow death's
celestial navigation. I look through this horizon of crosses
for the intersection of sign and fact, where you look down
upon the hearse idling for your body, where within the chapel
I imagine you seeing me thinking this. . . . But my faith,
like the church's, cannot locate the truth in *no return*,
the vanishing point whose base geometry remains unlearned.

8

What smoothness hides the real difference? If I were
smooth all the time and wore my crown like blankness
through the dirty streets I'd have reason to forget myself.
But I spread myself thinly, unevenly over dreams
of fame, the just ones. I've always believed myself
and you. I've cut myself into little pieces and fertilized
the moments with blood. When I leave my body and
my life is the memory of real places empty with sunlight
will the shadows accord in darkness over the remaining
faces? Will they see my absence as I feel it now,
throbbing in your vice, unlearned, torn between eyes?

9

The ceiling's open for investigation: tightrope walkers
above a netless fall bore themselves to death.
To make it happen I sit below, neat with patience and a
cold, calm eye. Why am I thinking I was a bad child?
Can it matter what I was before here? I don't blame
the country or search old earthbogs for a general clue
to a broader madness so am I safe in the smug
acceptance of fantasia? What do I see just now? History's
jaws opened and entered by a smaller beast, the searching
crypt-man? No, an indifferent thing I will call conformity—
the shape of a fairly smart guy—who's fooling who?

10

Bent limbs crane-white through morning rain drip
to slant ponds. A ripple to the sod, dead getting
dear, gone. Time taken to know the usual is the
strangest. Maybe nothing is worse than waiting for
it to happen, what stiffens or turns skyward unknown.
Why do things twist more and more? Contorted life?
Time of changes changes nothing. What's new? Another
touch, resolute distance from all bending, stiffness,
staying in rain, moving in sun to darker places?
A shape I share, costing nothing, worth only the
time it takes to prick an ear, pray, listen?

11

For my Candie Auntie I wept monkey tears and
climbed on her burglar bars all night long. I sang from
her Broadman Hymnal, rested on her broken Steinway,
cursed her printer's visor and yellow newspapers. No
matter how hard I tried I couldn't belong as she did to
the vine-rich grounds where the stone frog spouted
green water on days like these. I couldn't wax her cold
black floor or pull those bare bulbs' strings. Did you
leave stained bedpans, hoses and spouts like riddled
veins? Did you fill the room up with stench and die
muttering something about dues? Did you kick?

12

My vision's no deeper than these fingernails; arced
like their grime; rutted in bruises and words I won't
cut off. Only the look is clean, softer than life of
words or nails; life itself, forever growing.
If I could remember the color of
nothing. My life is everything moving out and curling
back in dreams within the night coffin. But I'm not
dead. I move more with present fear than future.
This way nothing stands out and what's unexplained
muffles morning, afternoon in mute surprise. I like
this better than funeral-going, blindness and closed eyes.

13

This morning I spilled my juice trying again "to
get it right for once." In the process nothing more
was completed than another swipe at what would dry
in time. I lost something falling through my
pants, graceless perhaps, but uplifting. I stood
out of place, saw where I just was: here I am, above
dust, below stars, choosing how to become and all
along it didn't matter what I wasn't or even tried to
be but what I was and couldn't get up from; all along
the only importance was that express notion complete
in spill, *ennui* or minor victory—a moment's awareness.

14

The day is old and solemn now: white-hooded icons cast
sun shadows through leaves, grates and stained glass:
. . . . water babies in broken windows. . . . Solemn,
deep light from light: distillate: ten minutes past the sun
watched me whitely watching elders on the Lord's path;
something foul shot through and I was the sun whitely
watching this whitening man before nothing. Who am I?
All things revolve in turn. No answers. Eyes line the
mirror wheel. Reversals are hubbed and spoked nightward.
Pinecroft Road ushers hearse and headlight mourners
through leaning trees. Distance, royal. We lose to see.

15

I can't stop writing the chants. The old-time curiosity
persists. Less than life, the myth struts soft-shoe by
the emerald stream. Keys in the green water, clues in
hidden colors—what matters? Gold memories spin
fast to something lighter. My head's a vortex drawing a
conclusion from the soft, quiet center. I can't say
it means I've found the answer but cherubic flecks
continue entering side rocks. Seeing this from
the six-foot tower: green behind blue, a horizontal lull,
pilot stars, dual receptors of the great mush, a throat
noosed tight for hanging songs. Dead man, who are you?

16

I am lit no longer by one useless image made useful;
I am lit by the imbalance of many images. They ramble,
they fart at will. Sometimes on the closest stage they
perform their stubbornly beautiful acts: they are beautiful
because they are stubborn, because in each refusal to
become a grander stage they force me without
much pressure to assume nothing: I have made the vain
connection of beauty and sunset: I have dislocated the stars
for a "broader context." But I will never again thread
the space between their motion with direction. I will never
broaden my horizon. See how the new one applauds?

17

Paradise has no child to wipe his nose in the tv night,
no callico wrap, no songs to sleep or gentle push like
Mama's crenoline arm into rugged dream mountains, no
thread for the perfect sewing of torn church coats, only
the chill drone—a madman's voice-work. Will you listen
if I call you beautiful, beautiful? Will you purr if I
stroke the mantel, the moulding in the dark hall?
Will you come down in first fallout snow and make me
forget? I have raspberry fingers and a clean, wrinkled
touch. I have seven closets of mysteries, four shoe trees.
Like the child, I'm useless.

18

Life as landscape: winter common empty and white,
raw maple thin as a stick, crow almost swallowed by
endless sky. I am of this earth so long I feel older, like
what rocks may rest beneath all, free to remain, frozen
to the center, hidden. How, why my body came to this
realness only the wind knows and if I hear its way
I follow. Is there one window with nothing beyond,
one silent and close enough to faintly feel? Life as mind-
scape: frozen chimes, once a mirror, hang in the garden
reflecting only scratched silver. Day, day, if I tell you
what I love will you turn and listen?

19

On the God matter I waste no words, only money. Today
I silently bought a holy book illumined by the angels. I
read my story quickly. To all forces locked in spheres, to
thin shadows tied to circles I told the rest: a star escaped
last night and fled the sky; beyond unread time he flew, past
difficult friends and harder theories he hurried; and sometime
near twilight, on the smog-thick field I saw his heritage
through electric towers, screaming. His ghost swooped
down and as quickly was gone. He who once barely lived
to tell more than any here now circles the loss, screaming.
In the grace of night and live wires he barely waits.

20

How many years before I learn old ways in loose gray suits?
The little night man in the last afternoon dream hobbled
by, singing.
Can I catch him if I give up running after the next fall?
Can I remain naked in ten-mirror four-ply carpet rooms?
Can I forgive myself for thinking I will never think beyond
the crucifixion of thought? Rilke, who thought himself an angel,
really, would scoff if I told him my foolish gray errand: I must
move beyond fortune, into the azure settlement with the elders;
I must tell them we are all angels, *really*, but *not* scoffers,
with little time to worry and less to be happy, with time to
remain
in spite of it all, easy with our option—we don't need wings.

21

Pressures of this unregarded life send me out for air.
I rise above what others will or will not sort out.
Sinking, rising, I stay in place—a smile in the
window guarantees that. But there are bristles in my
back and a summer wind stronger, longer than any I
remember. Am I all right or is it a useless battle?
No, not that. I can shoot the sun and I'll always love
slipshot loose on the table, notions filled with holes.
That's my life, I'll take it. I won't die until the word
demands I drop with this tone. Now? I have
colors and smells and a brand of truth that listens.

22

If I die tomorrow the radio forecasts a similar haze.
If I die tomorrow in this coil of human exhaustion you
can believe me better for the exit. What man is truly
believed by his fellows in the life-head? Man inflicts
upon himself his own mental debris; soon, what he
sees is diminished in other eyes because he sees so much.
When his flowered brain wilts sevenfold only to burst with
rotten bloom tomorrow, it's difficult talk of yesterday.
Unbroken chains! The body drifts in the circle called hope,
to be out, but form remains. If I live tomorrow I'll rebound.
The spirit will know my voice by the silent sound.

23

We know how to love when no one's close. When the
spirit trills beauty might as well be a whore. We'd
rather mess around with the new sister of pain and play
with the cards of neglect. Like choirboys in late afternoon
cathedrals a change in light makes us laugh at the saints.
We run home whistling a chorus for stains. Houses
topple, governments fall to their knees—it's a matter of
attitude, they tell me. Yet the mind's an airplane, and
love the air that propels. It's easy to move through air,
love, but try stopping for a breath of light, as a friend
stops another friend on a corner for an answer.

24

I, like you, want to feel the concrete base of the untouched.
I want to run my hand along the gritty edge of future,
giving to that surface my real skin. I want to be a part of
everything I cannot feel, touch: the betweenness of the mean,
the idea's quotidian, the simple fluid in the non-word, coursing.
I ride my bicycle by a stadium breathing like an invalid,
filled with the langour a crippled news bendor radiates in an
arm chair.
I prefer the complex sensibility of cocktail talk from corners.
Am I becoming a recluse? I tune, rearrange time-worn patterns.
I lunch on cliches, dine on puns. Right now, mind out,
I repeat my blood-tongue on a cue from the television:
what's on?

25

All these shelves and forgotten books—what do they hold?
The forest? The dream? The forest god? The dream self?
Love from each sinful beginning? Nothing? Like Magritte
I sometimes open my head to ordinary afternoons
and my thoughts become exposed, run loose through hay-light.
Sometimes I'm nearly stripped by my hard ordinariness,
but it keeps me panting, harmless, another throat in
the human zoo. Down-cage dumb-dressed bones are viewing.
I'm surprised they're this far in. They can't stand the touch
of truth and love stinks if it stays around their great noses.
I know a man who died touching everything closed. Where is he?

26

My right eye's cool, my left warm; my right eye's open
to the possibility of coolness and meter, my left closed;
my right eye is as beautiful as the sky, my left ugly;
my right eye sings the song of sun-devolution, my
left only feels the dullness of the day; my right eye
breathes itself into itself, my right eye shoots vision
into the mirror, accepts reflection selflessly; my
left eye only mutters with its lashes "Nothing
matters as long as it's clear I'm no good"; my right eye
attracts the glances of beautiful women in shopping malls; my
left eye strays to the left, and further, into its socket;
my right eye is beautiful and free; my left eye sees.

27

Though it's only July the autumn heart slips in a
dying reminder. What tempts me this morning? the
way I easily remember time's rightness, those alignments
with myself, watching football games, coaxing a date's
profile to love my direction? All that: the beautiful
leaves, one different from the other yet the same; the ugly
streets empty of themselves, corridors to winter winds;
the early mornings when I woke up near the walls, pushing;
the later afternoons steadied by bourbon and easy chairs.
Sharp break with light: blue on blue past meridians, blueness
of mind, I guess, those swept-up places crinkly with shade,
haunt and shine, waiting for autumn and beyond.

28

It is time to brake sunset, void calm, spur water to wave;
it is time to upset the balance of things relieved in corners;
it is time to open hearts to thoughts of nocturnal ovals;
it is time to circle the page with chalk-blue dust flying slow;
it is time to inhale the last cigarette expecting another breath;
it is time to lose the connection, pattern the void on vision;
it is time to lose the vision, to blue the loss, to control nothing;
it is time to blend the joints in mush-devotion to cornball;
it is time to run through streets emptying windowboxes, spitting;
it is time over tea to tell your mother you have lost, finally;
it is time to face your self in the faceless present.

29

Journeys are nothing but slantsongs. In rocks, voids,
windnooks the music spirals within/around. On the
granite no monumental face in bas-relief, just wind coolly
presented to the several grooves, whispers and silence
moaning like a graveyard hound, nothing
to say in a chimney rock, just thoughts of you and the
stovepipe life (the spirit-draft). In the other life
I stood around too. I picked and scratched and shuddered
while angels flew with the birds promising nothing but shit
from the hum called sky. The stakes were high, the fires red
and horse-rent flesh later rooted in the cracked streets.

30

What went away with the silver dollar sun? I lay
down calm, unblinking. On the slate-smooth ground
my mind is clean and hollow, glistening. When I want
I belong to the great beyond—past that
it's up for grabs—but as sure as each phrase turns
into suspense this mystery grows. The miseries, like
puns, shed their outer skin and the raw, shucked notion
roots for meaning in a fodder of new words and groans.
Feeling, always present—a whorl, khaki-strong, full
of space and undone useless suspense. Significance?
meaningless but for wordless protection and love.

31

Somewhere in blue distance a few eagles sleep in thin
pine beds. The space between their dream slivers and
my mind is saved for the final flight. There's always
a place for terror, for leaping into the heartmouth
moment where nothing matters, where nothing can be clawed for
relief. Under the lowest rock I look at my denseness
and see black, porous. Sponge man, watching hidden
eagles nest in my mind! I'm too far from their true
gold wings to fly but I see glory. The angels never
leave my eyelids. I will hear thunder,
I will roll with the clouds into silence.

32

On a Paris street just off the Seine I saw death in the
eyes of the unconcerned. They would have dipped me in
their still, black river if they had known I was labeling
en masse the French Face. I was afraid. I thought I
would lose my way and stumble into the hidden *Musee
des Revelations*. They couldn't have cared less, or
so I thought in my camel hair coat, swallowed up,
faintly in love with the clay colors and the unthinkable
way each statue retained its due balance of history. I
was inclined to breathe a prayer I knew: *Je ne parlerais
pas en classe sans permission. . . . je ne quitterais pas. . . .*

33

Proportions of the whole, free dream of desert-watching:
yolk caves dance; each show lengthens the certitude of
nostalgia—take dark laughter spilling over the frothy,
white slopes, accepting the sun crazily, deepening to shade—
a joke muffled but passed on death row: "Where are we boys
that time says no clean or quiet place is beyond this?
What attraction of zebra lights gives us even the freedom
to dream of death? Is the mind-tree more real than
a past crime or the world a cage we have to craft closed,
accepting? And can we reach through? And will there
be a final touch so deep the blood will boil out, free?"

34

If there's a story in the stars let the stars tell it. Let
the moon that looks loud-mouthed tell me how it goes on
and on. I'll listen. Accordingly, I'll write in a pad
like a newspaperman. But if the stars choose to wander
through their holes and the moon clams up from too much
investigation then the absence will make a much truer
story: how light gets lost in translation,
how the moon turns blue from touch;
how on days when he calls himself the poet the man
wanders into the woods for a closer afternoon look: he
loves to examine his body in the broadleaf shade, silently.

The Dialogue, Part One:
35
"It's not my kind of poem. Within each line there seems
to be a kind of frantic despondency, a fidget, if you will,
a turn from fact to antic that completely severs my desire
to continue. I've read ones like it, not exactly, but
similar enough to remind me of the present poetic fallacy—
he doesn't care about revision! From word to word it's like
reviewing on the drawing board some ill-prepared subdivision,
a place in mind I'd never inhabit, not even visit. As for
the sketch, he has a gift, I must admit, and further,
even now and then I get the intimation of a structure.
But the finished product? I think he ought to be a
window washer!"

The Dialogue, Part Two:
36
"I'm your window washer, sir. Do you dirty windows?
Perhaps a pane or two that needs a little wiping, for nothing,
so you can see through? Yes, I've worked for people more
visionary than you, but rarely do I ever get to work for one
with so much insight—I was recently wondering: what
do you do at night? I mean, after the lights are out,
after it's past mattering whether or not the panes are clean?
What do you do when you can't see a thing? Do you wonder
about black or do you close your eyes and with your back to
your brain feel faint throbs, your 'human engine' I believe
you call it? That's my heart, sir. Daily, I wash it."

37

And to those who say "He isn't Blake" I say I take
what's mine, not his—the proof's this line, my will.
I survive as line and flow into the next with the joy of
that word joy and the other—words after words,
sacrificing nothing but what's whittled by space, shuttled.
A pile of sweat approaches from New York. "Where's
Faulkner?" he asks. Don't ask me. He goes south.
I stay in these shadows building word-blocks from Liner-
notions, vision or Wittgenstein. But the line hums true,
blames nothing, keeps to itself and will never be spent.

38

The luxurious decadence of the International House of
Pancakes is my social coefficient. Unlike Proust's
petite madelaine I get off on red syrup swirling down
buckwheat lamina while Old Golf Husband's
two steps beyond Hale Mary, wif. My nose fills
with mentholated vapors and Certs' deluxe. I smell
a past quivering like steam from the stainless shelf.
Coughs circulate under each checkered table when the
50th anniversary couple splits. The velvet mouths of
the Matador, Flamenco Maria and Father Antonio drop.
Take me farther back, Sweet House, because I can't pay this bill.

39

The world's a strange place, so they tell me, filled with
the brightness of cheap food and freon—the usual cliches,
even this one, a note pinned to the chip on my shoulder: *Don't*
forget the people you can't do without or the love you've given
freely. Always be on the up and up. When the shit falls
you'll be in store for a square deal. You've got what it takes
to succeed. And after that brush with death you've bounced back
like a trooper! You're on even keel. Right on, you've got
the bull by the horns! Sure, the world isn't a rose garden,
but then you don't have to eat the thorns! Go to the movies
now and then. Let your hair down, Samson. A quitter never wins. wins.

40

My world is a small, smarting spirit. It has oblong
grooves for whispers and intricate Chinese boxes for sighs
within sighs. It has side-smooth bevels and learning notches
and dovetails signifying my twice-risen moments above fancy.
Lately I feel it creak: death in the dusty underdrawers.
Death prods like a salesman I can't do without. I walk.
Last night I left my heart in a simple shroud. I finished
the dream sideways, by the white tub tile. Water ran from
my heart. In the clear stream I saw your doctor sample
his breath. You were dead. Was he proving he wasn't?
I woke up, stamped letters, organized papers, smiled.

41

No better time than now to tell the truth about
nothing, to tell no one but myself I have never
understood anything about anything or ever felt
I was qualified to feel qualified in this world.
Questions I try to phrase beautifully
the jagged answer of silence surely deafens;
and this is only prelude to the greatest fall,
when I come apart completely and someone else
sees pattern in my dissolution, and makes of it
the kind of sense easily repeatable in schoolrooms
where children grow like hangnails in the blinded sun.

42

In the sunset mirror my face is marble and cold.
Yes, this statue shaves at first dark, when dogs howl.
I am drunk on the absence of the heart who now rests,
his own frozen stone. This face of mine? a frieze
whose hands refused the pose called studious pain, trembling,
whose body rose this morning in the pericardium of fear,
numbly tripping from Bill Trotter's hard childhood bed,
drawing a shower in a child's fabled bathroom, where Fox
calls Rooster and the sun is blue like you.
God, give me this evening my evening stone
and I will dance the statue's dance all evening long.

43

Thinking of you, I forget you. My mind grows steady
like a child's, driven into itself by something scary,
soft, a gossamer scarf billowing from my mother's neck
in the open boat at dusk. . . . We ride homeward,
my father steering between deep green waves, pointing
with his duckbill cap to nothing.
Curled in the hull I smile
with sunburned care into his tiny eyes, he touches my
knee, *I have understood*, and we love, my father,
mother and I, before the water is crossed, in the
here and now, which is never so clear again . . .

44

As I grow older, and do not fear writing *I grow older*,
I grow shakier, and uncertain, and see almost everything
as *oh, again*, with no time for those scrutinies
that once clung to me like new leaves with eyes all
their own. Now I am trying to see my figure stripped
in late autumn, where a continuous wind blows this stalk
to every root and sends through all that I touch and touches
me the reverberation called Stand. I am standing, now,
without anyone, ashamed of everyone I tried to be, of
every thought that tried to surface truthfully, that I
choked off, afraid. I am afraid and proud of this
fear that stands in me; fearful of pride, Fall, Stand.

45

And that was that. He didn't hew his brave song for the
trees or dedicate his full, white moon-look to the dark
side of things. But for himself, now curled within the
dreamsheets, dreaming. For the blood's little flow now
still as space and storming, now echo: *Removed, unmoved
am I over endless shores, amazed, ignored, never whole*/
Then he looked, after his custom, through time to home.
No keys to leave, the final freedom. No grace, future
or wisdom. But love after meaning, its own resolve.
Love after cough, phlegm, blue tissue, calm. Love
after everything, its own resolve, its ending.

Post mortem:

*Old Guy Turned Wolf told me this: "Your ancestors leave
you a third nipple, a bent ear, a straight nose, gold power
sometimes pain-colored in a beaten dog's eye, a great smile,
the legs of a black man, the chest of a trapper, the thumb
of a rubbed-dull ax end, a mind's edge like uncut wood:
ringed are your dreams; the deeper you sleep the deeper you
go into the forest of hope where no man tells you his horse-
shit, where all things are those things, where prayers are
received when truly chanted down in our stink-bog, where
nothing reflects falsely in the eye of another seeker, where
the easiest turn from groaning sleep to morning is pleasure."*

II

THE IDLER'S WHEELS

1

I was told to move from the death of a friend
to something permanent like history. The voice
wanted it to happen through me so it could get down
to the business of ice where ice never melts, that
solid monument to what was and is always the
same block. This is a way of saying, the voice
said, it must be told like it was or it isn't worth
the telling. I thought of simple tales, where nothing
is told, a cat-look east, my breath in November
curling out the window, little cloud where I was.
I couldn't drive through intersections of the past

2

so I stalled on the shoulder near here, and slept
on it, that glassed-over look I saw myself passing
to a mannequin being changed in a mall window,
changed for a season that may or may not happen
but nevertheless stands naked two good shopping days
past Christmas, waiting to be dressed in the voile
its owners have been told will sell . . . once the
season arrives . . . and we are in that place . . .
looking at the same plastic shape wearing once more
the future. Will we ever catch up? I can afford
everything but the price. And what of that which never happens?

3

I say, let me sleep on it and I will tell you my dream,
where we met, and shook each other awake, and passed
on, never sure of it happening at all. That is certainty,
love, the fog itself, the thoughts after members of the
club leave the club and drive home, alone. Nothing is
remembered as wonderful, nothing is dismissed as
terrible, everything is a great back room we are always
entering, where early fields and shattered windows heavy
with parallel raindrops and a cow far off and jockey-club
cologne rest in bought-negligence, the disarray of space,
its lines earth-bought, hanging, gathering shadow, silence.

4

But we must go wherever we go, looking to our sides,
counting telephone poles, semis, bulls in clover, trees.
We must go there and be there and when we are there
forget what it was about this place that made us come
here in wonder. . . . Smell my shape. Turn me over,
inspect my hard shadow with your impatient boot!
Leave me black and white to rise forecasting the daily
weather! Cold, dear, colder. Warm, wet, milder,
different, what's the real change? Feel my forehead,
brother — this storm is dark but slight, my own wind,
a groove I follow like a trench below fire, little comfort.

5

Fear and love are like fluorescent signs hook-lit
on the stone copse of some farmer's cornerland.
So free of static, so passable, it's easy to see the
words when I travel fast, attracting a view of life
that becomes history as soon as it's over. Later,
no thinking begins, it's the same two-lane road home.
The difference is just a way of forgetting where I was
and going where I'll be, holding to the right of center,
watching the center oscillate like some needle attuned
to my real direction. Then I come into your world,
the bright halves of your town's extremes. Twenty seconds.

6

I passed right through, I am still passing over
those memories where I have never been able to remain
the one who worked it out to everybody's satisfaction.
It is not "somehow I left," because I have always been
going away from you, wherever we are, going to
another place as likely as this road which is the screen,
the moving account of what comes clear at random.
It must be my life, a place I cannot avoid which casts
itself boldly between these lights, cutting out blackness,
cutting in on the present like whip stall on a short flight,
going down with no time to grab my heart.

7

Since it doesn't end I must find the place to stop
or go on. Since I will not end I will go on finding
nothing. Since I find nothing and go on with everything
coming and going, since the words in my head drive
me senseless through states and signs and available
exits numbered white over green in orange twilight,
since I feel the journey, its low center swaying like
a map juggled in downslope, I will look for you, love,
because something tells me you are the only way to go,
the only way there is, the way that finds itself smooth
after fools like myself have passed over it quickly, still looking.

8

Look both ways before crossing. Take care of this side
before going to the other. Watch what you must. Don't
close your eyes before you have seen it is clear and straight,
a line you have memorized well, a line that pulls you
with the evenness of desire balanced by caution . . .
The sidewalk dips in a dream of fame. Before you know
it you are shaking the wind's hand and the pat on your back
is the street. When you look up your good luck is red sky
and you are floating down Mistaken River. If we had
enough time to trust our instincts we would not be here
at all and the crossing would gather snow without markings.

9

I crossed over the bridge into a gulf of neon where
a thousand moths silently whipped the high sign.
They drove home the thought of living nails beaten back
by attraction so hard twilight from Eden to Blowing Rock
must be gauzy with dust of desire. If I could see why
we must destroy ourselves in the face of that light
whose cool center will never warm us, whose hard cover
will never break, I would do the same thing I am doing,
and teach my children how to bust their heads, to relish
the cracks in darkness, to plan the next assault in madness,
to jam the air with the electric whirr of blind faith!

10

We have the gasoline of faith, so exhaustible it scares us.
We have our natural resources, our weak fire whose spark
breaks the constant gap, coughing. We have our ways to
get off, our well-planned exits, our cloverleafed entrances
to another world just like the last. We have our idling
rests. We quiver through the weekends in one place,
watch the rest of us go by. . . . We wave, curse the
passing hands tuning the long distance radio to a frequency
so close we know the sound is traveling music dear to the
heart of journey itself, that syncopated beat, soul-wax from
Motown, the motor city whose sons have survived
putting us here.

11

Then we are in the flow, discharging our energy in the
pole-filled night. The lines shudder with early frost and
good intentions. The ramps release new shots of light
like urgent ammo from a pinball machine. We hit our
marks! We are there, putting the machine to sleep
in a good friend's garage. He has given us his bed
and we are grateful. We sleep on the floor but our wheels
gather tork in the centrally heated stall where not even
the Siamese cat is allowed. Our car dreams of the
morning when it can bring us into a new awareness of
itself, more certain than the last. We will love that.

12

Someday when you are impossible to live with,
when your dream girders sag and you meet
the dipping between sleep and light, when you wave
in place, when you see your dance tight as a turban
around your skull, you will fall in love with what
kills us all — sludge stronger than kudzu —
manifold exhaust nicking cylinder, leaf, lung —
no random accomplishment; just what happens,
what goes on; and you will want to know what shade
of that certain moment you can call friend. Death
will push you to your breathing eye, racing screamer.

13

Death will twirl your twirlies and gobble your gook.
Death will manage the children, the day, the bills.
Death will give you time to watch television slanted
by remote pushbutton, and you will see why you are here
if you are going to remain, and THAT'S ALL, FOLKS!
after Three Stooges will sign off your reasonable skull.
God, I cannot play with your life, your dying, your
living, whatever you are to me now! Once I tried
to live off death. I couldn't get past the front gate.
Now I'm writing about cars and death and nothing stops
me on the interstate like a cop to tell me slow down.

14

Lord of this road, look after me when I am gone.
Stand on my shoulder, turn your head this way, that.
Understand why I pass you, when I do not see you,
why I am faster when you are near than when you are
going the other way. Lord of this light, this time
before changes, look into my eyes when I am looking
to avoid you. Trees, fields, houses, people tell
me I will meet you when they are gone. So, now,
when I am nobody who needs you in rear-view mirrors,
let me see what's there, so long in this body waiting
for the real sign, the multi-colors, that way, not this.

15

Lord of this house, whose doors lead to slick streets,
whose windows let in rain and cold, whose walls release
the dreams of my love and my hope, whose morning floors
stand my weight as it walks across in fog so thick the vision
is hidden until now, Lord, builder, destroyer, driver,
walker, I will build you a temple and call it I-29, my
age when you read this black across white, when you
get around to reviewing my case. . . . I was a rich
child in love with his image, one to slight mother, father,
the day itself, who rode a Dyna-flow Buick to private school
and learned algebra before he was ten, who won debates

16

arguing affirmative for the space program, who hid
in his pinewood bed above transistor music from WYDE
before it was time to pray for his salvation
and all the relatives, who talcum-powdered his nine-
year-old torso with clown shades for his father's Rolliflex,
who holds that photo now, wondering about the bullseye,
the canteen, the door to where it all led — to here?
Lord, you know better than I. What do I stand for now?
Your occasional scribe? No. Your listener? Maybe.
How am I supposed to know what, that's this refrain.
I'm asking what I feel — this dance of life across my roadbrain.

17

Because my grandmother was out there I gave my breath
three seconds' grace and went under for you — Southside
Baptist Church, Easter Sunday, 1962. When I came up
Dr. Jackson in hip-waders was the face of joy and I believed.
Three times in five years afterwards — to 1967 — I re-
dedicated myself to a cross and the intersection gave me
little time to question — I was moving — that's an answer
to half the problems our dear departed never answered.
I died in May, 1972. I arose. Now I am electricity
numbing its charge against an outlet called world. I
flicker, I spark. Once I saw the colors of release!

18

Once I forgot I should be kind to everything. I forgot
I was part of everything. I had my phalanx born of
hate; to get through was my edge, to freedom. I
was free four years and died in freedom so pure
I called the straight-jacket Brother. I woke up bound
to the world of progress. I accused every eye of
selling out. Two nights in the twitch of thorazine sleep
I struggled to die. The road never left me! I got
solarium freedom with fast talking. My orderly told
me about fish in the Warrior River. Where is he?
I love that morning, the still orange light of nothing!

19

No luck holds. Grace falls side-still in the ditch.
I pass humming a tune no deacon knows. It's called
"Faith," friends, in simple exchange, line-on-line,
passed through bars to stomachs where even heat holds
long enough for drunken eyes to see why we're here.
Obscure? The best felt across cold muscles gathers
friction, while the bones warm to the marrow — something
we dislike about traveling anywhere — all the time — stands
out — but pain stops it up and we take it in stride, singing:
"Oh Holyanna of first choice, this bustling tune seasonal
dressing! These flushed cheeks calling fire a spade!"

20

The shapes of love blow backwards in the wind;
all different, all the same, past empty corners,
homebound friends and into the silence of the latest
field, a vision of white express, the past . . .
I am going through a skid. In motion's hammerlock
the evening is eternal but I squirm like a floored wrestler
to be free. Of what? Where is one space, a puny
nursery-grown tree plunged half-assed into the ground,
whose limbs like needles swing backwards to light,
to grow . . . *there*, sucked in *there*, consumed by
light eternal, traveling slant, up, getting clear

21

but this confusing undergrowth of weed and thorn,
going *there*, not here, *there*, which we will all
overlook because by that time it is all over . . .
what budged, gave in, sagged, spurted, curved
through a thousand well-harbored itches and pains
to this static bloom in late December which is no
more than a sand castle raised by an idler's child?
Why must I follow? To find you passing out the
drinks, pouring out the salvation, telling me It
doesn't matter? I'm sick of thinking about the route!
I want to be where I can sleep really doing the right thing.

22

The ass, the fool, the turd, the shit, the fart,
the lamb saying I am frozen oh Lord don't you care
about our entrails, me being your meek half who
only cries beautiful words when he's pinned to the block?
Hear me, Lord, the whine is ageless so they say,
the fear solid like Peter's third denial, the source.
We are founded on the illusion of shit — we stink
and love it. We don't know who we are or where
we're going and go there thinking we've been there
before . The newest hair on the lamb's cringing neck
is filled in every follicle with more truth than we deserve,

23

will stand the cleanest split of all when the ax falls.
So what of us, loud drivers, churning flyers who
give nobody the chance to get in? I know what —
we've got what *we* deserve! We shoot through the
easy way out, to make it somewhere near next to warm
moma's downy neck. This has all passed in early
minds, the hitch, the joke across the picnic table.
We cannot get truth because we deserve the ghost
whose form consumes our love. We miss the higher-ups.
I know a tale called Loss. It flies. It lights.
The desert wears its marks like bar-side Indians' dribble —

24

like America's centerlines the sand is riddled with scabs,
flowers, rivulets of time deep in the central flush,
Canchernoz' wind. Printed souls, a map where every-
one folds, sleeping through love's convoy, wheels so slick
they rise above the steppes, waltz over the bottomlands,
never hear the sea we listen to when weather allows.
The rush, the horizontal drive ever-climbing to un-
known plane, the oval view between walls of comfort,
into the big whoosh, the suction-gap we prod with toy
swords of intellect, hoping to spear one piece of
whirling body so far into distance we only see a cross

25

when we should not look at all . . . this river in the
bottom of my glass is far enough from anything known
to offer sign; if I could only see what I take in each time
I breathe to the wall of my senses. I rebound, dumber
than before, more attuned to hint of star, the slight twinkle
of stomach poised   lotus comedian this joke   cold
laughter on the cow's fourth belly   laughed up into
the grain eaten by stewing truckers on the Atlanta-to-
Miami run   good God, what is going on? How far is
habitual before psychotic? Exits are hollows covered
by paper minds — get me through this linear grind!

26

26 roads on a young man's chest, ho-dee-ho,
which way does he go, which one does he reach for
in sleep's knot, which rope does he hold to as he falls
for the millionth time into the gray zone where bubbles
are faces and love semiglobular like oil over water
refusing to melt? 26 lines on a young man's face,
ho-dee-ho, which one does he cut, which one does
he hold as life itself? 26 ways to go, ho-dee-ho,
and many more as pert as the plague. 26 lies, 26
dreams, 26 numbers all in a row and a bottle of rum
to make it go down easier, deep in a dead man's chest.

27

27 down and more to go. 27 ways of looking at
too many morning blackbirds to count. They rise,
quivering solid triangle, into the easy sun. They're
gone. Oh, zee life, the French films say, where a
man drives a car, smokes a cigarette and eventually
finds out some piddling thing about himself, like a
mole turning to blood in black and white. How can
he be sure it's blood and not a black liquid called
Illusion seeping from his heart? How? He knows,
as I know, smoking like he smokes, looking out my
window like he looks out his window, into the still eye . . .

28

Countdown to freedom: exit blast, moog, cyberfurnace;
enter silent plinks on A-man's wheel, diddle-de-diddle-de
ploooss. . . . Turning humm, convergence of semicone
and star, zloooop, out the vents, into air supercharged;
diamond policies bought by young men burn in the yellow night;
cautious policemen tweek moustaches behind the lights;
every driver is careful to feel his way as his way and no
upstart punk blasting down the exit will make him angry . . .
We must watch out because we are being watched in this
tandem hour. All our dreams converge in the cloverleaf
of stars and funk. We will get there because we are gone.

29

You won the prize in their eyes because they saw you
as a man at ease in the coming-home landscape.
Where you had run away from everything into oppositions,
now you were showing how "beauty can be simplicity"
and the easiest thing is perhaps the best thing after all.
They awarded you a road you already owned, and not
just that stretch before them but all the past they
never saw. How timeless that you just happened to be
in their front yards when they were in the process of
elimination. How beautiful that they gave you everything
it takes to be heard and seen except themselves — because
you never needed them and they were used to you by then.

30

I have never won your love because I do not go
that way. An easy face to be, the culmination
of desire and syntax, the hard moments in the shell,
all this sends me away, smiling. If I mute shadow,
love-talk, stillness, I have this fear standing out,
strong emptiness so much harder to conceal than see.
In the seasons, in every way weather can be and has been
and will be, there is no need for this. I would be
swooped up in the time if I stayed out talking like this,
if I didn't stay in here thinking of ways to leave. The
days and nights, the roads and houses, the lines to each,

31

the sudden disclosures of weakness in workers' eyes,
the way they are somehow physically ruined by fear,
cut to the marrow in a second, opened up by my eyes
which see themselves in their turn-of-the-century mirrors,
which claim these reflections are useless, spendthrift thinking,
ways to waste a perfectly good day. If you have an
answer like love-as-medicine, the antique elixir guaranteed
to spell your absences when you are gone home blue,
then I must tell you I have taken it many times to look
again at what was a moment earlier the look of when.

32

When will it all be fine, when will it all be fine,
fine enough to taste, fine enough to eat, to digest,
to live like this constant pressure to arrive? to see
right before the other immediate thing, to see beyond
the road into the darkening volume I have not entered,
only imagined when I am bored or scared or both or
nothing definable as that. . . . There is a way, straight
down the middle of religious books, looping through
the minds of the never-satisfied, which is the journey
itself, the burden taken lightly, but not glorious or
an end after endings — an easing beyond questions,

33

like a year in the sun of the sunniest place on earth,
where you soak in what you've always wanted while you
release what you've never been able to lose for more
than a dream. I'm talking about talking yourself to
peace, behaving like a dead man on a stretch of sand
that the road led to because you had come this far and
it was no longer possible to go any further without dying.
Before you know it you are thinking of rivers in the body,
this broken dam and a flood of sweat blasting away
the impurities . . . or is it the other way, and you
are losing your resolve, what brought you here in the first place?

34

I do not know but sometimes I am determined to be
formal with myself, to set myself down at the long,
polished table and invite the invited possibilities to speak,
to tell me as politely as possible what it means to be
possible but never something you can count on, like
a rude servant or a bad meal. When Rimbaud wrote
"*Les anciens animaux saillissaient, meme en course,*"
he must have meant after this gathering of nothing,
when it is no longer possible to be either polite or
possible, when the only thing to do is to do it like
it's going to be done if it's done, or to forget it

35

and all the qualifications I've gathered, six at the
setting, to throw away and finally go Blah-blah-blah,
brother universe, let me alone, leave me in this mess!
I can get in my car and go somewhere new
enough to feel I am neither old nor planned, a hummer,
and if I do not go, if I do not do it, if I do not forget
it, then I can inspire the ancient beasts to rip off
their long black evening clothes and join me in the
rotten ribs of pleasure, and we will eat our way out
into the early morning which would have never been so
beautiful had we not destroyed ourselves beforehand.

36

The soul in my body has taken me forward and left
me on the edge of December 22, the official night
of winter. I am holding myself close, thinking of
my soul, of saying it finally in coldness and not worrying
about saying it anywhere, this fellow who has always
veered to one side but been around as he is now,
who has always seen to my largest needs, like life,
and left me alone to take care of the rest. Diminishing
returns, an interstate of lights going both ways, the
souls I've never known whoosh by below the bridge,
Exit 121, and I can hardly believe people feel anything

37

moves them where they're going. Member of this
madness, a gone rusher who's bound to see his share
of travel to nowhere, I can make sense of life if I
only forget it matters more than love of space and silence.
I love these times alone, not knowing what's next year's
progress, the certain days abandoned like fruit stands
on two-lane highways. I love the quiver of neglect,
the trembling fist of doubt which grays a shredded bill-
board's frame, the tentative chirp of quail you must
slow down for and then disregard as meaning, the new
fluorescence like a halo over the sleeping suburb

38

as you leave it alone in the freezing silent hour,
the mashed dog's luminosity at first light — transcendence,
fidgit, gas to smog, blows received, given in transit,
forgotten, little battles, graves in the air, echo — —
halo — — drift — — drizzle — — purple quvering — —
standard routine — — let's get back into the swing
of things we have always passed and go to, this churn
lasts! These sings are standard — what time breaks in? —
I feel like a big meal, mama, mash me some potatoes —
I feel, I feel, I — — the particles of going, the stinging
way you must turn all ways to escape into a pocket of hope

39

where you are finally bored. Who needs an extended
vacation to nowhere? Why not feel the ices, the melts
of minds into traffic beyond control, weather, numbers?
You can be fine in the accident, stutterstepping to avoid
a woman's mountain of steel. . . . You can live here,
with me, if you want to. I spring up like a dreamweed
in crowded corners. I live here. The calamity is many
of us sharing space, the friction of missed hands, no
method good enough to apply. The wonderful way.
I am a truant lingering beyond these doors I cannot forget,
the learning place where everything will be used as long as it can.

40

Don't forget you are meant to survive the boredom,
our fierce animal of faces and houses who stalks
in place, never letting you forget your heritage is now.
Everything human before us is gone. We are what has
arrived and what will disappear; what briefly holds
ground and sky; what tries to leave; what is kept
where it is force of the force, helpless.
Don't forget you are surviving, or that surviving is
boring most of the time and the rest is memory
blown out of proportion, walking like a priest down
altered aisles which cannot be restored by faith,

41

which cannot lead to salvation or damnation,
which lived as we lived it — once — and is now
living without us. Pale summons to nowhere! Light
in my heart refuses to melt! I can tell you what
to do, I can tell you what I have done but I cannot
tell you why it means go on and do it again, different
this time, but do it all the same. All the same is
always distance, the hawk's hard balance over road
into his nest, the plowman's gumption to plow,
the defeated runner limping like a soldier across the
track to a metaphor in the shower which will not explain

42

this huge need to return the gift of extinction.
Oh the shadows charging across the development,
a dark red sun above the sagging power lines,
the smooth new road into everyone's garage!
The wind is a villain now because it has broken
us into silences and will not come back to be punished.
We beat on the walls because we are alone,
but the simple truth is we are everywhere,
and beating out loneliness is the code of getting on.
I hear you are shy and will not agree to love.
That's allright, you go ahead blotting out references

43

and I'll go on making poems out of sagging power lines
and maybe somewhere near Unifax, Minnesota, we'll
meet and look out the clear, double panes and see
a face in the snow. Hope is as close as fear. Why
not shove your hand through the homosote and come back
bleeding? Good God, woman, God is great and loves
the scars of desperation! How can I talk for you?
I am looking at dual scars of rammed-through love,
twin rises of clear white skin over both thumbs. I
broke a window. I crawled on through. That was years
ago, before fear. I'm still crawling.

44

I'm still turning over, still climbing halfway up
and falling back in my grooved-out place. I'm
still sleeping here. . . . To ride a dream of peace
soon becomes less important. To want more than what only
fades with the sun across acres of parking lots where
my shadow extends into darkness, returns smaller
the next time I am here earlier, longer if I am later
and winter has passed like a billion shadows into spring.
But winter has gone nowhere. We are relatively stuck,
aren't we, rubbing thoughts together for fire . . .
and the unknown image curls into a cloud over our heads.

45

All past recedes: rondure of hill sluiced to drain,
dun of leaves curbside heavy with three storms.
I'm driving home. I know it like cousin John Robert
knows Philadelphia — a book; closer, two pages
open and easy motion down the middle to a place
with a foreside view, the free zone where all is
received and accounted for and duty-free, just there
for the taking or the forgetting, held to stillness
by time's hasp, gathering a realness it resorbs
from living's steady air. I've driven myself here
enough times to know something is driving me.

46

I've returned, to wake up once more, skinny
with desire, quick to counsel every rising in me
that goes into the world from my heart . . .
Life to you all, those stars from my vision who
now dance alone, and those of you outside
looking to make your own sense of it, behind your
dream windows, who avoid my rattling wheels,
who stand beside slanted mailboxes in another sinking
universe, beaten sideways into that muck by time
which crosses all lanes illegally, never caught
but always catching us when we are trying to reach love

47

or a friend who will listen to how we will do better
next time, or at least learn, or at least not make
the same mistake, nor fall for the same hard luck story,
or . . . something. Life to us all, who continue
this Christmas night beyond the adoration, into
the following day, the assumption; you whom I cannot
know and hardly describe, but who are in me now,
who have goosed your earlobes to feel only life,
who live in gauze, who wear gauze, who will not
forget the way you looked beautiful in an uncle's mirror
that hung in a poorly-lit hall that ran down the center

48

of a house you visited on Sundays, who now waltz
from room to room, leaving a trail of scarves, ties
and studs, who draw elephants on medicine cabinets
through the steam of three-hour baths, who sigh a little,
who drink more than is good for you, who send pecans,
who receive clues from the mesophere, who tap on
the marble lampstand after coffee, on the first morning
after everything is over and nothing but the tapping
is begun, after a night is over and the last day is only
four miles you drove in and four you drove back to this tingling,
this chance to recall what you have given and received,

49

what you have stolen, what you have promised
to return. Yet we are all complete, hewn not
from roughness whorled with stubborn knots and warps
care cannot remove, but the smooth thing, the finish
we hardly feel, that space we own which patiently
gives us room to declare our imperfections rule.
It is not like that, nor simple, nor straight result,
but a wish convolved in the pure blood, rolling us on.
What I'm trying to say is already said. What I want
to know is the offing's plan. So I take the old-line,
join my senses' cue, stand with strangers all night long.

50

From memories spring forecasts. Sand stings waters
I will never see drowning my love, but I feel it now.
The present is an idler wheel, the largest of three circles,
the other two, connected, being past and future. Presence
is greater than anything before or after, the center where
we are thinking this very moment of ways to make its
constant turnings smoother. But presence is supportive
of itself, its guide and contour from all that happened to
everything else. There is no scale down to simple reference,
no easy way to blueprint desire shuttling from me to you
because it never happened that way. We were always

51

out of it, and so we may remain. But if we ever
come close, and feel something like all time in our
bodies as they move to the new degree of certainty,
a more sparkling, terrible this, then we must step
back, never join hands again, because we cannot stay
where we have never been. I want to tell you how
it may be but I do not know. I want to rejoice
for everyone who has stepped through this sliding door
but I do not know the sound of enter or return.
I am going on. I am going to see the world again,
those places I have passed and will soon see if I am there in time.

III

LOVE IN RETURN

To Cricket – all of it and everything else

1

Love comes from death relived in idleness.
It pulls me from the tunnel and shows me
the mountain sinking effortlessly to receive
whatever faceless season it will wear.
When you came to me with love in your eyes,
when you circled me in easy shadows,
together we looked back across the love-sky
glad to not see this had ever happened this way.
There are children in our eyes now, long, smooth
children of the future. Their clear cheeks blush.
In the pure wonder we stumble towards them, together.

2

Like the children we were but cannot become again,
we try to remember the grace-ways we followed
through this world of edge and halt, this newly broken
mirror reflecting every mistake, distorting every favor
we have granted hoping similar return.
When will we learn one sweet evening is enough said
of beauty, the thing itself? Will we ever be glad
to court misery as we now dress for gladness?
With our hope divided by our sorrow, can the rest
carry us through the zero days?

3

We die while we shuck the husks. Sometimes
we find the kernel is small and brown, loveless,
a seed half-blown before its prime weight balanced
the force of earth. We have come up early
in our lives. Our skins are still raw
from being torn from what we were. But together,
coarse in the bed we have shared through five plantings,
we know the feel: we are borne through time
loving and hating the ride we ourselves allow.
What we have lost comes up green and we see it
as the landscape our twitching bodies manage to meet.

4

I love you alone when I am alone and your eyes
leave your face to shoot out slowly towards me.
I am seeing you become the bridge through distance,
though distance still surrounds. I am with you!
Time smooths out pain with your single span;
once more, love takes over. If we are warped
by our selfish visions of each other, if we see
our shooting eyes gleam to passing travelers,
we must learn that love also is a vicious whorl.
Within its curves are hates and desires we cannot
choose, that choose us, forget us as we pass.

5

I have seen you toweling your body so many times
after showers I love the rain I walk in without you.
I have seen you powdering your face so many times
I love the dust I walk in without you.
There are so many things you have done in time
with so many things I have done I am in love with time
that moves us in its own way towards a place
we will never know together, which one of us remaining
will remember as love, the world behind the love
that moved two lovers through it until, at death,
the two are the same, and the one of us who walks

6

away from the place where the other one rests
will shortly follow. Love, as it was said, close
my eyes when I am gone. Love, as I say it now,
press your mouth against my eyes and see my love
for you. Even in death it shines through what
has passed and will remain on your lips forever!
There is no stopping the force of love. It runs
like water through fields four months without water.
It runs like water over streets five months without cleaning.
It runs like water over dams newly broken.
It runs like your tears, and the tears are the waters of love.

7

Love lives in the circles beneath our eyes,
the circles around the moon before morning snow,
the circles stray snow dogs make sniffing garbage,
the circles of sense we cannot make, the nonsense,
the circles of doubt we cannot see through,
everything silent circled by days and nights
as we circle in the great gyroscope, safe in the center,
waiting for a bump to throw us off. We cannot
survive stillness but no one will move us.
We will wait, our arms circles around our hearts,
and we will breathe as one small top whirring to end.

8

When your eyes will try to meet tomorrow as today,
when you have seen that you are looking for a face
whose look is incomplete, do not turn against yourself;
for the face you cannot see is lost, content to slide
below memory into the tunnel of darkness
that first brought you here. You cannot recall what
will not finish the decomposition. You must hold
my arm and kiss my neck and feel my slowing blood
as yours, because as we move through the silences,
as we count the haze-times, we have counted the times
only time remains reaching back briefly for us.

9

And if love falls cold between the walls and mirrors,
if love becomes a mouth always whispering lies,
will I crawl to you with confessions and dead talk?
Will I somehow change our mostly light hearts
to window weights sealing the beautiful clear panes
from two hands touching light outside together?
Love is guilt on the edges; within its frame we walk
and crawl and lie still looking out on the universal fuzz,
the ends of eternity's cheek hairs so close we fear
one touch of this blushing godless smile —
our faces after love-words, when we first loved.

10

Rain's freezing eye forces us to the fire,
and in its flame we stare for our future.
We mourn the lost sun as if it is gone forever.
Each fleck of ash returned by wind into our gaze
sticks on the slate before it disappears.
We huddle in a time we cannot renew, nor hold
even now as it warms us in its grasp. We are
small, unblessed by every dream, reaching up
like the smoke for a larger place to move through.
The love that rises in this silence surely returns
to warm our bodies, to tell us we must go on.

11

I cannot go where you go at that same time
or even be your arm's counterweight over space
enough for one to fall. I can hardly hold you!
When your face is clear motion against my breath
I feel you gone, dancing on the dead man's bridge,
foot-to-toe exercises of grace above the endless flow.
But holding close, if far apart, brings me reason
to follow these zig-zag shadows. I did not come
this far to love the day, but to love you leaving
not me, not love, nothing but life in the non-month,
on the non-day our minds drag the memory stream

12

for the body we share to lose. I did not come
this far for this much, yet now I have it and loss
nicks this monument. What time are we in?
Have we passed the worst hour? Is this the "finest
hour" or worse, the cliché called LOVE IS?
Questions of future never end. The skinny blackbird
we never fed hangs around so we can ask where
will he be in better times. Surely not with us,
not with anyone, but alone in the feeding time,
his narrow circle above the plants throbbing with
a little heart-wind; his mind on one more approach.

13

So many dead days hang like forgotten socks
on a black woman's frozen line. She, like us,
has gone to the city to hang new socks on old lines
in the attic. Each day we have lived together
is left where it remains, but if we go back,
hunting for the warmth we shared on foot-loose
days, we will have to free our fancy on the
journey itself because no feet remember love;
they carry us from wool to wool, true, but
the trip gives our walk its plumb and the only
thing out-of-kilter is the path rutted by rain.

14

Love is silent. The eaves carry January sleet down
the copper gutters. Our restored Federal Period columns
creak. Three spiders encased on the iced tile porch
wait in their still black suits to be swept away.
These melts, these ruts. We go on, watching. The
sky is gray. A dum-de-dum sings in my velvet ears.
We are older in this spell. The hand-in-hand roads
do not remember our rosy walks, the sentimental trips.
Merciful God is a nursery rime. Lightning sparks
a wireless pole. We watch the Architect of Grace
tear down the little arms in the field. Who sings?

15

Love is loud in this silence. Its wires unite,
flickering over the seasonless pole buried in my
straight-up head shocked to vertical recognition
of the dream mysteries in this waking life. The
three a.m. blues take many shades from many
shadows. They give a place to lovers separated
by sleep and eyeless hate. They shelter jealous
fists and thin white blood straining through seconds
spray the face like winter seas. When it
ends and the body drops, too exhausted by love's
wall to reach over, the mindless night is fifteen minutes louder.

16

If love dreams me dead, if my body cannot feel
in sleep what love has dreamed me, let me die
to be where our single hope lies. Smothered in
the backknots of time beyond understanding, stepped
over by everyone we have avoided, I will gather my
lost self in the gray basement. I will swirl my self
together and reach your light on the wheels of my
new triangle. Three corners will flash in the dust.
The light will wall-up. Love will shape our promise
and flower under the steps. Two children will
find us near the furnace, and they will build by our heat.

17

When I do not know love, I know you love me.
The strange separation is breath on another day
not able to fuse our minds in glory. But one of
us burns, refusing to live without the love
that smiles in every corner we know . . .
White heat after you go out and water the red-berried
bush called pyracantha. Berries for the birds,
early morning scatterdip of caw and scratch. Some
unearthly things dreamed last night, this morning's
haze, and January is hidden in the circular track,
the running haze, the running haze — oh so much —

18

Love has me saying what comes out. So long
I tried to say what I thought expected of me to say,
expected by those I did not know, whom I expected
by the grace of learning to love anyway. No!
The learning room is filled by nothing after nothing.
The nuns are a thought, praying for everyone.
I skip. I dance as I must. If you cannot watch
from the sitting wall, shake your finger once
and I will come over, and we will dance cheek-to-cheek,
and when you have taken the lead and carried me
in sleep to morning I will carry you in morning to sleep

19

and we will sleep there under the invalid's quilt.
We will kiss off palsy in the dew. We will go
slowly past factories streaming endless smoke.
Every mistake will be made once more in landscape
good for nothing else. On the edge of the plain
we will tell it all, and the blood-trees will blush,
reawaken. The sky will dance, yolks in a blue
bowl. We will drink the rotten sun and bruise
our tongues talking into scraped night, eagle dawn.
Between every edge the haze waits. There is only
so much you can do about life — but *so much!*

20

You can cry, you can laugh, you can hem and haw,
you can break and mend, you can take the high road
or the low road or the road in between, you can sit
on your ass and count the times you've stayed put,
you can go. If you go, take this with you: *there
was a girl who suffered like a stone; each time she
was dropped she rose again; like some hard-assed
Jesus she found herself grooved in the palm of the
throwing hand; one day water ran down her slope,
she claimed a man had squeezed her dry; when she
looked up she had already been pulled from his drowned eye.*

21

Why do we see what we see? If love is the eye-
chart's smallest line do we memorize it before
we take the chair? Love in mind is clearer than
what's here. Love described is never as clear
as that inner haze known so well for what it blindly is.
If I could really see this bottom line staring back cold
at me in open daylight, wouldn't I hope for
some new blindness to shine on the shadows we cast?
I'm telling you this: come against me in the dark;
rub my body with wordless friction and we will swim
in darkness' balm before we see the day again.

22

In the dead moments when love's failures
line my vision like Arlington's unknown crosses,
I see myself walking between the rows, love's
easy mark. I would lie here forever if I had
fallen in the course of action. As it stands,
I am the vertical source looking for your horizontal
flow. In dull winter hours, when the thaw
pulls the hardiest flies from their sleep and the water
cannot decide to freeze or ripple into the perk,
I too cannot go just one way. So you are everywhere
slowing, increasing the journey, shining.

23

There is no careful way to approach your love.
You see her dressing in the shade-drawn bedroom
at nine in the morning and by nine at night she's gone.
You spend the evening with a ghost of your desire.
She stirs, and her body contains the Louvre prints,
the thermostat, the tiniest blisters winter makes
across the blue ceiling. You enter the air.
What to make of all your closed eyes see?
Is the season of death repeated against your lids
like a watermark, the *fleur-de-lis*? Is your iris
flecked with the blood-shapes reason makes?

24

I slide to the edge of the carpet you had me lay
beneath our bed. By your vanity, I swear this is not
what I bargained for! You dress your eyes for sleep.
I notice the way your reflection powders in the glass,
nothing more. What I wanted was you, but I have you.
What I want is an answer to this suffering. Why do
I love you at all? The smallest bird flies with his mate.
When they love, in time, the egg itself departs and
something new flies through these skies we have so
long avoided. Love tells the lover:
make your words clear before you go.

25

Love's forgetting place is filled with lint. I sleep
on the shelf, in cotton underwear, dreaming of
love's staple, forgotten. Love gives me sleep.
I am covered by the looming. The early years
that weaved me now impassively watch this thread
disconnect itself from the fuzzy ball. Love lets
me watch the world spin on and on. It thickens,
thins; the colors whirr in the seasonal deluge of
water and dirt. Love is the way I never see whole
unwinding. While I constantly thin-out, the world,
in love with its shape, is the whittler, extending.

26

Easy to love gathering no details like harvest,
no certain ways to live on through this winter.
Easy to forget just how you became mine
when the moment's fluid and we are presently
all places we have loved, reaching all points
of the endless compass from this specific center.
Right now we have what brought us here, a love
sweeping seasons into pigeon holes, months into
corners and days into days not lived. The edge
we always cross extends itself. We climb the
razor ladder. We stop for the moment. We dance.

27

We dance the dance of the slipping floor. We
slide over the tilted universe, each motion
in grace an affirmative extension, life high-stepping
down the endless parquetry, into the gorge.
But the floor rises as we fall. It has always
been this way. We are always climbing in rhythm,
plugging into the handholds, saving ourselves
even as we wait for the last dance when positions
disappear, when directions disappear, when all
but love has never existed.
Dance called *"Dance of The Dry Hill in Evening Clothes."*

28

Kick your smooth right leg into the air and begin.
Take the shaded livingroom by storm. You are
electric and I am plaster falling from the force
of the third mare-stomp. You could crush me
into white dust and vacuum me up. You could
twirl me like a cane. You could forge my willing silence
into ballroom brass and I would sound your time
even as I was your red carpet. . . . But your
love excites in me parade rest, the jittery
stillness of a line of life-thoughts waiting to receive
the charge command, the exit into battleplan.

29

I am always ready to talk of love; its gauntlet
ribs the face of day expecting no clap-trap; its
spear rises through power lines. The word is
carried: we cannot live without knowing by means
we hate . . . *we love*, and all intent, aroused
in wide range through this web's binaric overflow,
points to itself, and loves itself and those it
happens to cross in the humming day. If you are
cut down the middle, pare yourself to the word;
love the world skipping over you and you will be
sucked up, inexact, but one clear part will remember . . .

30

Only living gives me a way to see death. In life
I am split by you, received by you. In your body
I warm to death and will not be stopped by it.
You clothe my halved self in the pride you generate.
From your warmth I spit and spark these words
and in your cooling shape I will understand nothing
easily before we sleep. The love tent stretches
over the rocks and dumbs the outside air to meaning.
Each word I hear, coming through your center-pole's
edge-space, tells me how fast through-love passes.
I catch its little storms in my palms. I blow out the light.

31

Love flairs and fizzles in the dreariest field.
Almost nature itself, the smoke through stalks,
the ultimate forgetting breathing earth commands,
we walk round where we lay in love, fired
together, tranquil even as we melted sense away.
What lets us alone? We who love most behind windows
look beyond the ruts at windows — people looking
not at us, but the other way, within, where some
single task like shucking commands their minds
and the thoughtful lovers crossing their land
are part of a night they will never see . . .

32

Building the earthly paradise on weekend time.
Walling the wall so the wall doesn't fall on in
and we float away with the animals in the flood.
Dum-de-dum said again, spirit massing quickcrete
against the body's mold, digging in Sunday itself,
breathing in the underdraft through rusted latticework
in the basement. The heater hums the heater tune.
It is all working, I believe, to the first degree
of getting things done. The body mechanical
turns its screws and the placements hold, the
lights come on, you are beautiful above me, humming.

33

This old day blinks and the sky comes on,
ordinary orders from the usual clouds, signal-flag
crows spell flash *yes, you take it like it comes*
you take it like it goes. All over the world
creaks and sighs and nasal giving-ins to more
of the same. Rise to fall! Rise to fall again!
Mindless love in bodies glad to feel love at all,
the blanks cancel themselves and hollow wind
blows fear into history's dust-bin. We are like
each mindless thing we see, given its life
as we watch it disappear within our shifting boundaries.

34

The courage from saying "courage" is a way
to watch my love become this thing that continues
to be warm and unknown. What spirit in
your blush, your up-turned tits, your mouth
pooked for a kiss above the hot-air vent!
Courage comes from what I see, recorded
eternal dalliance doodling its line over these minutes
passing even now into time's reflexive contrivance.
We have put ourselves up to the task of love.
Its business occupies our waking hours. We
sleep to meet what we look for in this light.

35

Everywhere stronger minds are stringing words
on threads, capturing chords, flattering equations
to turn truth their way. They must see what's here
so they break through and build another weeping wall.
I have love to do. No supreme man fits in this
master plan. Give me the gut-lorn moment, the
drunk's face drooping from every problem time creates.
I will dance on the pole. Somehow these ends
will turn. I will fall and that will be a master plan.
One perfect hexagon of ice will shatter; my bloody
cheek will oil the axis — that's how things get done.

36

The accidental love is surely life's only perfection.
A stunned man's bruises favor the blow, every
mean slash its delicate cut. Love is reprinted
by hate; the colors we bleed make our shapes complete.
We are meant to lose and take. There is no option.
We are strangler, neck, the last cough, our own
eulogy stuttered, lost in the long smog. If we
must correct what's already done we will be forever
ruining the immaculate prints we've made. We
must not rub out what's always below. Listen to
the red mole move through our solid black tunnels!

37

Strike through the boards of the printer's walls!
Send word-splinters into the cold! It's January,
writer! The world waits to feel your fist, to
soak your studious blood in the quiet snow.
The stinging air nervously anticipates your power.
Why keep living with the choices you haven't made?
Love melts the fear-road. Take your lover
to the dead end; stand securely on the striped
barricade. Your lover is your balance.
Look at what's still beyond — where you've never
been. Remember everything out there — go there —

38

The first step after the last will not fail to produce
the next until it is over. The first breath flows,
the last breath follows its own expiration. You must
always leave yourself behind. There is no other way
to love, to go. To simply love is always going
with you where nothing is so simple.
You will always forget you are gone in love to no
greater mystery than the eternal motion love makes.
The body is never coming back. On whose behalf
do you remember, forget? You are only what you
never reach in love, yet always in love with that.

39

Never held so close before. Never breathed your
neck breathing love like this when we first met.
I squeeze your wrist to feel your heart. You bite
my ear and listen for love from my throat.
Our mis-matched bodies jam in perfect union.
There is no mistake. This is what we come for,
starry reason shooting through our closed space
finally opening for prayerful sighs of release.
We cannot wriggle through — there is no other life,
nothing else to put off, get out of, go through.
I am not here to verify, but I know this is freedom.

40

I know I am here to tell you love is here.
Every precious object has its ingrown clutter,
its grimy underside and some of the beauty kills,
and that is love also, the killing, the recoil
from too much spring sugar, the viper's out.
I know I am here to tell you love is hard.
The language is not to be understood as fact,
yet penetrates, its own diamond drill, into
the diamond where all is smoke and mean dust
up in the eyes of you who search this far in . . .
I know I am here to tell you love is there . . .

41
You are the star-bringer in February mud,
thawing rock and root where you go lighter
than light itself, over every known thing, into
the distance. Your shining trail folds out
over unplowed land and split-level energy homes.
Farmer and banker alike are startled in their sleep.
You move through their dreams like forgotten children
on All-Saints Day. The see-saw tilts when you pass.
The jungle-gym creaks. Something human beyond
life makes you chance when they wake. "What luck!"
they recall over coffee, their concentration lost.

42
What they don't know will kill them. Listen:
after the statements are accounted for the man
in love with giving knocks. He doesn't want
a letter of intent. He won't take a longing look
at your wife's pocketbook. He'll say, "Don't
ask me what I come here for. I'll take a drink
and leave out the back door." Then he's gone.
You still have time to multiply what you have,
to divide it into what you owe. When you'll pay
up only you and the business knows. You'll be
in debt for years. Show your love, man!

43

I will never write my love for you the way it is
silent over hills with no name or recent height.
It creeps off, surrounded by my breath, thick
as my heart, its own world to proclaim. But
love is not senseless. We meet each day with
all we cannot tell or even understand. The mysteries
caught in our throats weasle out and the landscape
is new again. When I am afraid to tell you even
this much, so much left unsaid, so much said
poorly, I see the two dogs skinny with desire.
They have no strength. My mind barks for them,

44

knowing it is for us as we run silently down
the shady side of the street, into comfort, the
fire's tame end. What can be glorious but love
unafraid to speak its relaxed words in the time
when cold wins new and beautiful stillness?
With so many frozen friends in the corners
we must thank love for giving us this motion,
if frantic, through halls and parks that would
without our blessing be filled with creatures
and not simply idle persons. One word for the
deaf, the blind, the dumb: you are not alone,

45

no matter how many glorify your loneliness. In
your silent blackness, in your idiot calm a
greater voice sees you pulling love from your walls,
a greater voice than mine or anyone among us.
A greater voice pulls us all and as we drift,
reaching for the switch, the phonograph to come
on, we guard our silent flow. This is the voice,
the love I can't get right, the thing itself.
It is not so bad to be misunderstood by mortals.
You only have to hear your self laugh and that's
all. Cackle, crackle goes the fire, your soul.

46

It has not been easy figuring the ways I must go,
have gone, am in you. Where is always
hard. No enumeration of desire now, just the
slowing fingers used to snapping a count, the
blood-rhythm we share in this daily dance. I
give you my arm. You hold the trembling stick.
Never have you been so radiant across a floor.
What I'll never know of you makes me love you more.
Take me into the private room, under the chandelier.
I see we are going to stand close through encore,
release. You have no choice but my face in the powder room.

47

You close your eyes to powder my lids. You part
your lips, my mouth is red with accomplishment.
My back shifts to feel your dress smoothed down;
my legs stretch to crease your silk wrinkles.
You drink to my smile; I drink to your frown.
This is the way the world is done. What futures
are not bought on the present exchange? As we
get money for words written, parts played, don't
we deserve time to live out the combination plays
we know better than what the public sees?
In the third act the man has forgotten how to act
and blindly loves.

48

You reach an age where words are easy,
where life itself follows your own design
in afterthought, where things and thoughts
lie in parallel, cool on a sundial open
to any markings. Life loves light because it is light.
The time you reach proclaims itself found,
past. But there are other times, other lines
reaching out from your soul, ready to say
we are about to meet our circle in the black place.
Patience in these good times makes sleep crazy.
The sweat will come at three a.m. with the alarm nobody set.

49

Poetry ends up mattering less. The time I've spent
avoiding you is here. There is no more.
This is it: I love you in words from these silences;
I tell you what I feel. I turn my head, our world
goes round in the mist-branches a day past snow.
I'm edging down a time in love with you to reach
for more. I need you to keep me going. Now
the words are short, most of this brainlove spent,
but the praise is the life that has shot these thoughts
into place, that takes up your brown eyes and
lays them gently in your vision so nothing has been missed.

50

Death-praise wheels idle sorrow into present love.
Through you I was able to live death. The
idle days we shared grew thorns and blooms whole-
faced towards sun/moon, the graveyard chants.
I am thinking of what will come, of how it will
come of us into this world going on without help
from us or the dead. The line separates. We hold
hands on this side of the garden, looking through
our many satisfactions to the wall, the shore
where the running child splotches the green wall,
disappears into winter's slipshod prism

51

"and some without love" come up the lake to love.
I tell them they are the leaves still hanging through
this cold but they do not listen to me because they
are watching you steam the kitchen window with love
for me. All things dead and alive rejoice in your pattern.
Not hap-hazard, nor well-edged to fit all corners,
your love-breath fits the space we and our ghosts live,
and from this mostly-evening going-place a habit for truth exists.
In my words it tells you, Cricket, we have brought
ourselves here to remain together; each day we live
past uncertainty the glow we nurtured in our bellies
becomes the child we are making for this flow.

Tom Huey is a native of Birmingham, Alabama. He received his B.A. from the University of Alabama, which he attended on a track scholarship. He also holds a Master's degree from Hollins College and an MFA from the University of North Carolina at Greensboro, where he was a Randall Jarrell fellow. His plays, *Against the Middle* and *The Whitening of the Godwins and the Starrs* have been performed by ACT Co. in Greensboro, and by members of Lee Strasberg's Actor's Studio at the Circle Theatre in Los Angeles. He is married to the actress Mary Faran.

Designed and typeset
at Bull City Studios,
Durham, North Carolina

Printed in an edition
of one-thousand copies
by Braun- Brumfield,
Ann Arbor, Michigan

Publication made possible in part
by a grant from the
North Carolina Arts Council